The Twelve Best Questions To Ask Customers

Jim Meisenheimer

A Helbern Book

Helbern
Published by the Helbern Group
Lakewood Ranch, FL, U.S.A.

Helbern Group, Registered Offices:
13506 Blythefield Terrace, Lakewood Ranch, FL 34202

Third Helbern Printing, March 2003
10 9 8 7 6 5 4

Printed in the United States of America

Library of Congress Catalogue Card Number: 00 134585

ISBN: 0-9637479-3-2

This book is dedicated to my MSI colleagues and my best friends in the speaking profession:

Marjorie Brody
Frank Bucaro
Tim Connor
Lisa Ford
Kathleen Hessert
Mark LeBlanc
Bill Lee
Beverly Smallwood
Art Sobczak
Alan Zimmerman

You've really made a difference in my life.

Also by Jim Meisenheimer

47 Ways To Sell Smarter

50 More Ways To Sell Smarter

*How To Double Your Sales
Without Quadrupling Your Effort*

*57 Ways To Take Control Of your Time
And Your Life*

Visit my website: **http://ww.meisenheimer.com**

Blog:
http://www.meisenheimer.com/no-brainer_selling_tips.html

The Twelve Best Questions To Ask Customers

Contents

Part I

Selling

Part II

The Sales Call

Part III

Questions

Part IV

Staying On Top Of Your Game

Part I

Selling

1. The Selling Process

It's been called "the selling game." It's been referred to as "the business of selling." Many people call it the "oldest profession." What would happen if there were suddenly no salespeople to promote the goods and services created in our country? Nothing would happen; and that's the point. Salespeople are essential to our economic prosperity, always have been and always will be. That's the good news. The bad news is that there are lots of pretenders and wannabes out there calling themselves professional salespeople.

Some salespeople like Arthur Miller's Willy Loman, in *Death of a Salesman*, are always looking for brighter tomorrows:

> Oh, I'll knock 'em dead next week. I'll go
> to Hartford. I'm very well liked in Hartford.
> You know, the trouble is, Linda, people
> don't seem to take to me.

Willy can identify some of his problems like "talking too much," but can't seem to change. At the other end of the spectrum are the Ben Feldmans. I'll tell you Ben's story in

Chapter 7. Unlike Willy, Ben understood that selling is a process not an opportunity to talk.

The selling process is a template to use to achieve results. The selling process always begins with the customer, never with your product. The selling process includes asking good open-ended questions. It always identifies needs, problems and opportunities. Once these opportunities have been identified, it allows you to present tailored solutions. Usually, during your presentation you have to deal with resistance and handling objections.

The selling process also means, eventually, when the time is right you're going to have to ask for the order. I want you to notice I didn't use the word "close." I don't think it's about closing. We're trying to open the business, open the doors, and open new relationships.

It's not shooting from the lip. This process has an element of structure to it. Here are the key attributes of the selling process.

1. **The selling process begins with a network.** Years ago you acquired your list of contacts by prospecting. Today, what was once called prospecting is now referred to as networking. We used to gather up names and put them on our Rolodex. Today, our Rolodex file isn't a card filing system. We collect, qualify, and input our valuable contact information into popular contact management, database management, and customer relationship management software. The software programs

enable us to access and creatively work with the names on our list.

Networking is work; otherwise, it would be called "neteasying." Today it's essential that you network not only within your target industry, but also extensively within companies and organizations you're calling on. Companies consist of people. Because of mergers, acquisitions, and LBO's - people are forever changing jobs and moving. Today's decision-maker could be gone tomorrow. A skilled networker will already know the new decision-maker and will know where the old decision-maker has moved. Remember, the biggest and most complete Rolodex always wins.

2. **The selling process asks the right questions**. Today's contemporary salesperson knows that questions are more important than answers, understands that listening is more important than persuading and convincing. Asking the right questions is very important and it's equally important to ask core questions. These are tried and tested and also yield results. I'll tell you more about these questions later.

3. **The selling process depends on effective listening**. That's not an easy statement for a former New Yorker to make, where fast talking and not listening rule the day. I've discovered that effective listening consists of four things. First, it depends on your ability to ask rock-solid

questions. Second, to be a really good listener, you have to take good notes. Taking notes forces you into a listening mode. To the person speaking, note taking shows immense interest in what the speaker is saying. Consider the meaning of the word "noteworthy." "Something said, that is 'worthy of notes;'" actually, it's a formidable compliment. The third element needed for effective listening is to listen carefully enough so that you can record quotes in your notes. You need to record verbatim what was actually spoken, especially when it describes something unique about your potential customer. Later, during a presentation, you'll be in a much better position to tailor your product and service solutions. The fourth element is hesitation. Too often when a potential customer asks a question, we're responding before the question is fully asked. You can often show a genuine interest in your customer's question if you pause a moment to reflect on your response.

4. **The selling process also uncovers specific problems and opportunities**. After careful probing and acute listening, the specific opportunities usually become quite evident. Professional salespeople aren't content to speak in general terms. The identification of problems and selling opportunities is rooted in what the potential customer says, not in what the salesperson assumes. The more specific the

problem, the bigger the selling opportunity becomes.

5. **The selling process always presents tailored solutions**. Solutions that relate to the very specifics of the issues at hand never the generalities. The "relatability" factor is critical. You relate your product attributes and benefits specifically to your customer, and do it in a way that relates to his communication style. By listening carefully to the responses to your questions, you can learn a lot about individual communication styles. For example, you should be able to determine whether the potential customer is generally assertive or low key. You should also be able to assess whether he is task or people oriented. Knowing the customer's communication style, allows you to make adjustments to your selling style as you deliver your personalized product solutions throughout your presentation.

6. **The selling process deals with handling resistance**. At times, resistance can be quite intense, at other times only minimal. Eventually you'll have to contend with no need, no hurry, no money, and even no confidence issues. While you can't entirely eliminate resistance issues, you can minimize them by thoroughly understanding your potential customer. In my own business the less I try to convince and the more questions I ask, the less I have to deal with these objections - because the potential

customer is doing most of the talking. Remember this, a recurring objection is a gift for you. You can expect to hear it repeatedly. It provides you with the opportunity to prepare in advance how you will specifically deal with it. Take advantage of this gift.

7. **The selling process always seeks to secure a commitment** when the timing is appropriate. Nothing lengthens the selling cycle more than the inability to directly and professionally ask for the order. Clumsy attempts often rule the day and spoil the opportunity. Choose your words carefully, and practice them, then deliver them with confidence and watch your sales take off.

The selling process is indeed a process. At the foundation of this process are core selling skills.

Here is a list of core selling skills. Rate yourself on a one to ten basis, assuming ten is excellent.

_____ Telephone skills – especially for making appointments.

_____ Basic research skills – web-based resources.

_____ Questioning skills – especially using prepared open-ended questions.

_____ Listening skills –developing the art of note taking.

_____ Problem-solving skills – pinpointing customer problems to position your products as tailored solutions.

_____ Presentation skills – especially presenting to groups.

_____ Transition skills – segueing from uncovering customer needs to your product presentation.

_____ Value added selling skills – creating value throughout the customer development process.

_____ Handling the price objection skills – with prepared, professional, and spontaneous sounding responses.

_____ Time and territory management skills – on a priority management basis.

_____ Securing the commitment skills – preparing in advance how you will ask for the business.

_____ Technology skills - learning how to do more in less time and still have a life.

Any score less than a five should be considered a weakness. To achieve sales mastery and a quantum leap in your performance, you must convert your weaknesses into strengths. Learn everything you can about what's holding you back.   Learn to prepare and practice your way to success.

If you're currently navigating the steps of the selling process strictly on an improvisation basis, I encourage you to raise the bar with preparation and practice.

To avoid sounding canned, practice your presentation until it sounds spontaneous.

Food For Thought

The meek shall inherit the earth, but not the mineral rights.

J. Paul Getty

Well-timed silence hath more eloquence than speech.

Anonymous

Consider the postage stamp: its usefulness consists in the ability to stick to one thing till it gets there.

Josh Billings

2. Tools Of The Trade

What tools do you rely on to get the job done?   The salespeople I ask usually respond by listing their laptops, software programs, planners, pens, calculators, Palm Pilots, briefcases, Fax machines, pagers, and cellular telephones.

Here is another question: "What's the principal tool for all professional salespeople?" Guess! Guess again, and even take another guess and I'll wager you can't guess right.

What do you think the principal tool in selling is? I can't begin to tell you how often I ask salespeople that question. They guess and guess, and they continue to guess: it's communication; it's listening; it's product knowledge; it's experience; it's one thing or another.   And finally, I step away from the podium with my hands outstretched, and say, "I'm going to give you an example by talking about a different kind of business."

"Imagine I'm a potter, and I own a pottery shop." I hold my hands out in front so everybody can see my hands. Then I ask, "What's the principal tool for a potter?" Most people say, "of course it's your hands." I agree. Without his hands, there are no pots. Other tools include clay and water. The potter also needs a wheel, a kiln, a sharp cutting knife to smooth the top edge of the pot, and of course, a measure of talent. If you had good hands, if you had talent, good clay, water, a wheel, a kiln, and a sharp cutting knife, don't you think you'd make good pots? Most people nod their heads in agreement. Naturally, I agree with them.

Specifically, what then is the principal tool for all salespeople? In all the times I've asked the question, no one has ever guessed correctly. The most common responses are never even close.

For me the answer is different and it's simple. The principal tool is just that, a tool. Using this tool, you'll reach your selling destiny faster. Without this tool, selling takes on a different dimension including fewer sales, longer selling cycles, less rapport with potential customers and if that's not enough, it will hit you where it hurts the most in your wallet.

I believe the principal tool for salespeople is **words**. Our words begin as thoughts. We use words to formulate our sales call objectives. Words are used to get appointments and build rapport. The questions we ask uncover needs and problems are crafted with words. Once discovered, we attempt to fill those needs with our solutions in the form of our products. Throughout our presentations, we rely on even more words to handle objections as they arise. Finally, when the time is right, we secure the initial commitment, with still more words carefully prepared and practiced.

It's been said, "The difference between the right word and the wrong word is the difference between lightning and the lightning bug."

How important are words to what you and I do in sales? Most of the people I work with say they're very important. I believe words are the keys that open the doors to better relationships and to greater success. I have a theory about this. I believe three percent of what you say should not be a surprise to you at the time you say it.

Now when I say that, most folks chuckle. Most salespeople never prepare their words ahead of time. We often shoot from the lip. Many times, I know because I've been there; "we get mugged by our own mouths." I believe we need to invest time preparing the words we use during a sales call. *Three percent of what you say shouldn't be a surprise to you when you say it.* Ninety-seven percent of what you do can't be prepared in advance. The sales call is a 100% improvisation, if you are not prepared. Do you think you'll be as effective if the entire sales call is one big improvisation? I hope from this point on you won't think so. In selling, professionalism happens when preparation meets practice throughout the selling process.

The language we choose consists of words chiseled out of our inner dictionaries. To know in advance which words you'll use in a given situation creates a competitive advantage over salespeople who don't. Everyday you are judged by how you look and what you say. The words you use are more important than the clothes you wear.

The benchmark for professional selling will never rely exclusively on spontaneity and 100% improvisation.

Food For Thought

Talk does not cook rice.

Chinese Proverb

It is not enough to aim. You must hit.

Harry Truman

Imagination in business is the ability to perceive opportunity.

Abraham Zaleznik

Everyone must row with the oars he has.

English Proverb

We will either find a way, or make one.

Hannibal

3. Knowledge Is Power

The letters in the word "knowledge" have a special interpretation for salespeople. Why do so many salespeople face rejection as often as they do? To hear sales reps explain it, it's usually because of someone else's low-ball pricing approach. It really has more to do with knowledge. That's the reason. We often get no's because we haven't done our homework. We haven't properly assessed the customer's current situation. We haven't analyzed his preferred communication style, and without fully assessing his wants we often fail to demonstrate our real value. We haven't asked the right questions.

The knowledge you develop about your customers is in direct proportion to the success you hope to achieve. *To know is to win.* To assume is simply not enough to get you even close.

Your knowledge of a potential client, the key decision makers, their customers, their families, their issues and challenges, positions you in an extraordinary way to secure the commitment sooner rather than later.

Knowledge also creates a distinct advantage for you. Your ability to define specific customer requirements will enable you to differentiate your products in a more meaningful way for your customers.

Completely understanding those requirements creates the opportunity for you to demonstrate your unique selling edge in the marketplace.

Knowledge is power. Learn to leverage the power of your mind. To minimize the no's you get, seek to really know your potential customers in a way that creates a very personal and very powerful selling advantage for you.

You really have to KNOW your customers to avoid hearing them say NO to your selling proposition.

Food For Thought

The roots of education are bitter, but the fruit is sweet.

Aristotle

By nature all men are alike, but by education widely different.

Chinese Proverb

4. Upper-Hand Selling Strategies

Sounds evil, doesn't it? Well it's not meant to be. The buying and selling process are seldom a 50/50 proposition. If there is an edge, I believe it belongs to the seller. Saying it and achieving it are two different things.

If you want a mutually successful outcome with your potential customers try to gain the upper hand in these three critical areas.

Knowledge - Find out all you can about your potential customer's business, problems, industry, their customers and even something about their personal interests. The Internet makes this quite easy. Also check on-line magazines for what they're saying about your competitors and customers. An excellent source is www.ceoexpress.com.

Become a student of selling. Invest thirty minutes each day acquiring new selling skills and ideas that can be applied to your sales career. Create a file for these and related topics: time management, attitude, goal setting, negotiation, handling objections, closing, presentation skills, probing skills, change, telephone selling, sales force automation, internet selling, networking, etc. Read, save, and weave into your repertoire everything you can about these subjects and you'll see dramatic changes in your personal sales performance.

Communication/language - The words you use to ask questions, make presentations, and submit proposals paint a picture of you. When you speak, what do others see? If all your words are improvised on the spur-of-the-moment, you become the great improviser. Choose your words carefully. Learn to play with words, whenever you want to make a better impression. Create a list of seventeen power words and attempt to weave them into your sales presentations. Your words say more about you than the Giorgio Armani suit you're wearing. The suit creates an impression and your words confirm it - maybe.

Proper language is the real key to your success today. In addition to the above, you rely on language to converse with people. You use language on the telephone, to leave voice-mail messages and e-mail messages. The letters, e-mails and hand-written notes consist of well-chosen or randomly chosen words.

It's amazing to think, that all words are derived from the twenty-six letters of the alphabet. There is nothing more powerful and eloquent than a well-chosen word. Choose yours carefully. Think before you speak, and you'll sound like a professional.

Relatability - The role of today's sales representative is changing dramatically. Lone ranger selling is definitely out and team selling is in. Getting to know and being able to relate to large groups of internal and external customers is a prerequisite to achieving selling success today. There's more to the psychology of selling than knowing the features and benefits of your products or services. Pay attention to people. Discover what makes them similar and what also makes them different. Relatability follows understanding. You can't hope to relate to different people without attempting to find out what makes them tick.

There are three keys steps to being able to relate to a variety of people.

1. Real achievers know themselves.

2. Real achievers know their customers.

3. Real achievers adapt to their customers' styles.

When you combine knowledge, communication skills and the ability to relate to others you step to the head of the class. Remember:

- Don't be too busy to acquire new knowledge daily.

- Don't be too busy to prepare and practice your language skills.

- Don't be too busy to attempt to relate to all people, especially those who are different from you.

- Don't ever be too busy to make your personal growth and development your number one priority.

- Don't play the lower-hand if you want the upper hand.

Food For Thought

The ultimate inspiration is the deadline.
Nolan Bushnell

Diligence is a great teacher.
Arabic Proverb

When in doubt, don't.
Saul Gellerman

Behold the turtle. He makes progress only
when he sticks his neck out.
James Bryant Conant

Don't lose your head to gain a minute. You
need your head. Your brains are in it.
Burma Shave Ad

Everything is possible to him who dares.
A.G. Spalding

Spirited curiosity is an emblem of the
flourishing life.
Epictetus

5. "Value" Plus Selling

Value-added Selling usually refers to how you add value to your products and your services. Too often in our attempt to add value to our products we neglect to add value to something even more important - ourselves.

Value Plus Selling is how you increase your perceived value to your customers and potential customers. Here are the five key ingredients to Value Plus Selling.

1. **Vision** - one of the best ways for you to add value throughout the selling process is to have a clear and specific picture of what it looks like. For example, can you respond to the following request in less than a minute? "List ten ways in which you add value when you're working with your customers." Effective salespeople who make a deliberate attempt to add value can see it in their mind's eye. They don't need time to think about. Do you?

2. **Attitude** - is the great equalizer. Attitude is your most important intangible asset. It doesn't cost you anything to get it. It doesn't cost you anything to use it. It doesn't cost you anything to maintain it. If however, you don't possess the

right attitude it can cost you a bundle of lost sales opportunities. Very simply, your attitude is what you feel and what you exude. Nothing on this planet has a greater influence on who you become than your personal attitude. For those of you needing an attitude adjustment practice walking around with your chin up and a beaming smile on your face. It always works.

3. **Likeability** - people buy from people they like. People will even spend more money when they buy from people they like. One of the best ways to be more likable is to be less talkative. Take an active interest in the people you're with by asking really good questions. Your customers possess one of four dominant behavioral styles. And so do you. When you share identical styles your likeability factor rises dramatically. Whenever your customer's style is different from your own, you'll come across as more likable if you adapt your style to theirs. Here are several examples for you to think about:

- Not everybody enjoys chitchat.
- Some customers require lots of data to make decisions.
- Some people make quick decisions and others make slow ones.
- Some people have a time orientation that focuses on today and others have a time orientation that focuses on yesterday.

The quickest way to ruin a sales opportunity is for the prospect not to like you during the first sales call. Be quick to analyze your buyer's buying style and slow to impose your personal standard selling style.

send Advantage congratulations .

4. **Uniqueness** - it's been said "you can't run the mill, if you are run-of-the-mill." If you want to be remembered do something, anything, that's memorable and different. From this point on forget about blending in and begin focusing on standing out. Send hand-written notes, take pictures of your customers, have an annual golf outing bearing your name, add color to everything you do, send cards - birthday cards, holiday cards, anniversary cards, congratulatory cards, - download special interest articles and mail them to your customers with a personal note, prepare and mail your own e-mail newsletter, and do everything practical and possible to set you apart from all the people masquerading as professional salespeople.

5. **Excitement** - some people die when they turn thirty and get buried when they're seventy-seven. Some people walk into a room and suck out all the available oxygen, and other people walk into every room breathing life into it. Don't become a "walking dial tone" and think everyone will be attracted to you. Do you love the company you work for? Do you love the products you sell? Do you love your job? If you answered, "yes" to each question, it's

outstanding. If on the other hand, you answered "no" to any of these questions you must obviously learn the art of faking it or find yourself a more suitable position or profession. Your customers deserve to see you at your best. Make sure your eyes are sparkling when you're selling your products.

Remember this, you are a walking billboard. You are responsible for the message that's on your billboard. Your personal and business relationships will blossom with the careful cultivation of your personal billboard.

Think VALUE. Sell VALUE. Show VALUE. Add VALUE. If you do, your customers will see your <u>TRUE VALUE</u>.

Food For Thought

Beware of little expenses; a small leak will sink a great ship.
                                        Benjamin Franklin

He that does not save pennies will never have dollars.
                                        Anonymous

6. Do Whatever It Takes

What does it take to be really successful in today's business environment?

It takes . . . **Uniqueness**. Being boring, bland, and benign is out. Being different is your first step to being better. If you're different and you're better, you'll be remembered. Type "Inc." after your name. For example, "Jim Meisenheimer, Inc." Don't view yourself as a person. Think of yourself as a brand or even as a company. How are you positioning yourself? Create a list of ten things that make you different from your competition. If this is a tough exercise for you, you should invest some strategic thinking time. There's a fine line between ordinary and extraordinary, and you draw it.

It takes . . . **Passion**. Why do so few people really get excited about their work. How many times a day do you meet someone whose eyes sparkle as they are going about their business? Too many salespeople put their presentations into cruise control and expect the product to sell itself. Passion is the one small intangible that makes a huge difference in how you are perceived. Put a smile on your face; focus on your customer; speak enthusiastically and energetically; and go about your business and you will become passionate. If you combine equal parts of preparation and product knowledge with a splash of passion you'll take it to the next level.

It takes . . . **Discipline**. Every presentation could stand a little spit and polish once in a while. Don't get complacent about anything. The bedrock of success is order not chaos. Develop a system for getting things done. Have a system for planning your day, planning your calls and planning for your territory. Here are seven words. After each word add a word or two to complete the thought by personalizing it to your business and your territory.

Control _____

Prepare _____

Limit _____

Develop_____

Exercise_____

Restrain_____

Create _____

Discipline takes time and effort. Discipline is not being rigid, it's being in control as we work in chaotic and reactive environments. The choice is simple, *in control or out of control*. It takes nothing to be out of control. It takes discipline to be in control.

It takes . . . **Time**. You can't rush success. Success is not something you start with. It's something we hope to achieve. The bigger your challenge is, the longer the road. Most folks view success as the destination instead of the journey. Enjoy the ride and make time to smell the roses along the way. It's been said, "The only time success comes before work is in the dictionary."

The road to success is paved with a DO WHAT IT TAKES kind of attitude.

Food For Thought

One man with courage is a majority.
                                    Andrew Johnson

A good hearty laugh is worth ten thousand "groans" and a million "sighs" in any market on earth.
                                    Napoleon Hill

Don't complain. Don't explain.
                                    Henry Ford

He is well paid that is well satisfied.
                                    Shakespeare

Even if you're on the right track, you'll get run over if you just sit there.
                                    Will Rogers

The doer alone learneth.
                            Friedrich Nietzsche

The will to win is worth nothing unless you have the will to prepare.
                                    Anonymous

Always bear in mind your own resolution to success is more important than any other one thing.
                                Abraham Lincoln

Do nothing, and nothing happens. Do something, and something happens.
                            Benjamin Franklin

If I have a thousand ideas and only one turns out to be good, I am satisfied.
                                    Alfred Nobel

7. An Extraordinary Sales Talent

Most salespeople, if given a choice would not select life insurance as a product to sell. The usual jokes, the reputation of the industry, and the fact that it's been around so long, would not lead salespeople to think they could really make it big in that business.

You couldn't tell that to Ben Feldman though. Ben was eighty-one when he died November 7, 1993. He started selling life insurance just before World War II. The rest as they say is history. He almost single-handedly changed the insurance industry. He was just a salesperson.

It's been said that he didn't look like a salesperson, didn't sound like a salesperson, and didn't act like a salesperson. Ben was different in every imaginable way.

Here's some background on Ben Feldman. His family was Jewish immigrants from Russia who settled in eastern Ohio. At his father's insistence, he dropped out of school to sell eggs for $10 a week. He met Fritzie Zaremburg, a schoolteacher, who later became his wife.

As an adult, Ben began selling insurance. After selling insurance to all his friends and relatives, he then targeted businesses in eastern Ohio and western Pennsylvania.

27

Without going beyond a sixty-mile radius, he often sold more insurance in a day then most agents would sell in a year. In the 1970s, it was reported that he personally sold more life insurance than 1,500 of the largest 1,800 life insurance companies.

During his lifetime, he sold insurance policies with face value over $1.5 billion. One-third of it was sold after he turned sixty-five years old.

According to many, Ben wasn't ordinary – he was extraordinary. Harry Hohn, Chairman of New York Life Insurance, said, "Ben really felt everyone in the world was underinsured."

Ben believed passionately in his product.

Ben knew how to really "WOW" his customers. His words were his craft. According to Rick Hampson, an AP writer, "Ben would sit up late, crafting the pithy sayings that he called power phrases and rehearse them with a tape recorder."

Ben realized selling success came with preparation and practice.

Ben achieved one goal after another. In 1975, he was the first salesperson to sell $2 million in a single week.

He was goal focused. He sold life insurance by talking about life, not death. People didn't die; they walked out, as in, "when you walk out, the money walks in - the insurance money." Taped inside the front of his presentation binder were several pennies and a $1,000 bill. He would tell his customers, "for these," pointing to the pennies," you can get this" - the bill.

He was creative.

In 1992, New York life created an insurance selling contest they called "Feldman's February." The program was designed to commemorate Ben's fifty years of selling life insurance. The salesperson selling the most in February of 1992 would win a nice prize. The national contest was of course in honor of Ben's history with the company. It was assumed that Ben would not compete in the contest.

Apparently, no one told that to Ben. He viewed it as a challenge and won the contest himself. He was eighty years old and in a hospital recovering from a cerebral hemorrhage during the month of February. That February, he sold $15,150,000 worth of insurance from his hospital bed. He never gave up. He never, never, never, never gave up.

Listen to some of Ben's phrases and how his words became magical. Imagine hearing them as you consider making a decision to buy life insurance.

>*No one ever died with too much money.*

>*Do you know anyone who has a lease on life? It isn't a question of if; it's a question of when.*

> *Put me on your payroll. The day you walk out, I'll walk in and pay your bills.*
> *The key to a sale is an interview, and the key to an interview is a disturbing question.*
>
> *Most people buy not because they believe, but because the salesperson believes.*

For Ben, success wasn't fleeting it was a process. He believed in his product and he loved his customers. He also loved his company and his work.

Ben's gone now. His legacy, however, should serve as an inspiration to all who call sales a profession. Ben Feldman gave new meaning to an old profession.

Here are a few of my personal observations:

- You can make every year easier if you work harder.

- If you want to be remembered, be memorable.

- The quickest way to achieve success requires time to prepare.

- Focus all your efforts on the results you want to achieve.

- If it's important - think about it, write it down, then do it.

- Put a tape recorder into your selling toolbox.

- Identify the critical measurements of success for your business. Then measure them often.

- Establish clearly defined written goals if you want to achieve a higher level of success.

Food For Thought

Seek the lofty by reading, hearing, and seeing great work at some moment every day.

Thornton Wilder

The value of a thing is the amount of laboring or work that its possession will save the possessor.

Henry George

The toughest thing about success is that you've got to keep on being a success. Talent is only a starting point in this business.

Irving Berlin

Jim Meisenheimer

Success is that old ABC – ability, breaks and courage.
> *Charles Luckman*

Toil, says the proverb, is the sire of fame.
> *Euripides*

He who does not hope to win has already lost.
> *Jose Joaquin Olmedo*

Neither a wise man nor a brave man lies down on the tracks of history to wait for the train of the future to run over him.
> *Dwight D. Eisenhower*

Part II

The Sales Call

8. Preparation Is Essential

The word preparation is a powerful one. It has many meanings including: "fitting, making ready, rehearsing, putting in order, building, foreseeing, developing, arranging, adapting, and adjusting." It's truly challenging to be prepared for the many and various scenarios that may occur during a sales call. When I think of preparation, I think of putting something in writing. When you organize your thoughts on paper, your preparation has begun and a written plan will be the outcome. It goes like this. Think it, write it, and do it. The person most prepared usually feels the least anxiety. The person least prepared feels horrible.

Be Prepared
Be prepared – **to have priorities**. Priorities keep you organized and headed in the right direction. Schedule your priorities daily and you'll make better use of your time. Prioritize your accounts to optimize your call schedule. Your list is prioritized, if every item is numbered. If it isn't numbered, it isn't prioritized. It's that simple.

Be prepared – **to set performance objectives**. To achieve better results, carefully plan your objectives. Push yourself to go beyond the traditional sales and profit objectives, which are predetermined for you by your company. What are the critical measurements to your success? Once they are identified, you can establish personal performance objectives and action plans to keep you on track.

Be prepared – **to deal with a variety of people inside and outside your company.** Treat everyone with respect. Any time someone helps you give him or her an "Oscar." An "Oscar" is any word, deed, or gesture that shows recognition, appreciation and gratitude. A thoughtful gesture goes a long way in today's rat-race world. People are starving for recognition; it doesn't cost much to give them some. Be a master delegator. The ultimate sign of trust is to ask someone to do something that you know you can do better. Delegating will free up lots of your time and telegraph to people that you trust them with the important stuff. Doing it yourself is not a good strategy. It may even limit your potential to achieve success.

Be prepared – **to interact with different personalities**. The dominant types (18%) are very direct in their approach. They are brief and to the point and want to focus on the task at hand. The expressives (28%) enjoy interaction with people. They want to socialize and give you their opinions. The amiables (40%) seek harmony and structure. They are very patient and expect a logical approach to the facts. The analytical types (14%) want data and facts. They are precise and accurate. They expect you to be very thorough. You can't take the "one size fits all" approach with everyone. To be effective you have to be adaptive. Become a student of what makes people tick and your sales will increase sharply. If you want your sales to take off, adapt your style to the customer's style.

Be prepared – **to be passionate**. Don't expect your potential customers to get excited about you and your products if you aren't. Today, there is so much busy-ness, that few people genuinely show enthusiasm for their work. There's only one thing more contagious than the common cold, and it's enthusiasm. Learn to get excited and stay excited about your work. The shortcut to passion begins with a smile. Passionate people are always smiling. Let's see some teeth on your next sales call.

Be prepared – **to be persuasive**. Persuasiveness contributes to successful selling if it's timed properly. Nothing turns a prospect off quicker than a persuasive salesperson at the beginning of the selling process. Your ears will out-earn your mouth every day of the week. Persuasiveness should kick in only after you've completed your homework. Passionate persuasion can work miracles. Remember, not too much and never too early.

Avoid Seal Talk
Have you ever been in an audience listening to a speaker and suddenly thought "Wow!" It happened to me, while attending a National Speakers' Association Conference in Orlando. Joel Weldon was speaking, and he talked about "seal talk."

Seal talk is what happens when we don't prepare. We fill our moments of spontaneity with "ah's" and "um's."

As soon as I heard the phrase "seal talk," I instantly realized he was describing salespeople who don't prepare key words and phrases in advance. Whenever we are uncertain of exactly what we're going to say, we hesitate momentarily and fill the void with these delightfully empty utterances – "ah's" and "um's."

The choice is clear for professional salespeople. Prepare in advance. Practice your power phrases in your car before trying them on your best customers and potential clients. The goal should be to seek perfection in the way we communicate while realizing it will never be 100% attainable.

Today, being a professional salesperson means looking good and sounding good. You don't get a choice.

Practice Until Your Legs Are Sore

This is about a regular guy who happened to win $1,000,000. Here's the story. I didn't see it happen because I was on a plane to San Diego. The story appeared in a *USA Today* article in the sports section. I read about it the day after the Pro Bowl game.

It happened during half time. Dennis Crawford, a home improvement store manager from Cleveland, Tennessee kicked a perfect thirty-five yard field goal to win Hershey's Million Kick Challenge.

He won the Million Dollar Prize. He was one of 518,000 entrants. He was one of four randomly chosen contestants. He beat the other three and earned the right to kick it through the uprights for the million dollars. Luck, right? He was just lucky, you're thinking. Well, up the point his name was first selected, it was either luck or divine intervention. I'll concede luck.

"I practiced until my legs were sore." That was his response to reporters after winning. It had nothing to do with luck. He prepared, practiced and got the job done.

And how lucky must you be to succeed in selling. Think about how much better your results would be if you prepared and practiced the primary selling skills. You would increase your competence and boost your confidence at the same time.

Imagine the following. You prepare the words you want to use to make appointments. You rehearse them into a tape recorder. Once you have it down, you play the final tape over and over while you drive from account to account. "You practice until your *mind* is sore."

When it comes to meeting potential customers for the first time, you develop your approach word for word. You rehearse into a tape recorder. Once you have it down, you play the final tape over and over while you drive from account to account. "You practice until your *mind* is sore."

You realize how important questions are to understanding client needs. You prepare twelve questions, word for word until they are perfect. You rehearse into a tape recorder. Once you have it down, you play the final tape over and over while you drive from account to account. "You practice until your *mind* is sore."

You know it's important to be able to ask for the order. You prepare exactly how you will ask. You rehearse into a tape recorder. Once you have it down, you play the final tape over and over while you drive from account to account. "You practice until your *mind* is sore."

Success isn't limited to luck, though it may be a factor. It's about methodical preparation and regular practice.

Be A Movie Star
Next to closing a sale, the thing most salespeople dread is sounding "canned." The word "canned" brings to mind those products that come out of a can. Whether it is vegetables, fruit, or dog food, "canned" products of the same brand and type are all supposed to come out looking and tasting exactly alike. Quality control departments pride themselves on achieving this "sameness" goal. But salespeople don't want to appear exactly like the competition. Each salesperson wants to be special and be remembered for his or her unique attributes.

In the movie business the word "can" has a different meaning. Having the movie "in the can" represents completion. The film has been rehearsed, filmed, edited and is ready for distribution. This "canned" movie may bring us to the edge of our seats, cause us to reach for another Kleenex, or roll with laughter. The action that we see on the screen that appears spontaneous is actually the result of many months of work. The stars spend countless hours memorizing lines, practicing facial expressions, perfecting gestures – and yet it all appears spontaneous when we watch their delivery.

I listened to an interview with Pierce Brosnan before his first James Bond picture. He was nervous about following the legendary Sean Connery and Roger Moore as James Bond. Brosnan talked about practicing one of the memorable lines in all of the Bond films. The line has only three words. It's Bond's introduction.

Bond – James Bond.

All of us remember that line. We can even hear it when we read it. It doesn't matter which Bond we hear. We remember the intonation, the smug look on the actor's face, the confident but still nonchalant body language.

Three words, yet Brosnan said he practiced that line thousands of times. He said he practiced in the shower, in front of mirrors, in his car, at the grocery store – everywhere. Brosnan talked about the hundreds of ways that line can come out depending on the emphasis given to different syllables, the spacing between words, the volume of his voice and all the other variables that can change the spoken word.

Brosnan practiced thousands of times to deliver a three-word line, because he wanted the delivery to be perfect – yet sound spontaneous. How much time are you willing to spend practicing to sound spontaneous?

Avoid Sounding Pathetic
It's amazing when you read a novel how much you can pull out that you can apply to daily business and selling situations. In a novel by Arthur Haley, he wrote, "Salespeople are compulsive about filling silence with their own voices."

We often fill that silence because we are nervous, and that comes from not being prepared. I'd like to share a few of

these "filler" words and phrases that I'm going to ask you
to avoid, because when you say them they make you sound
pathetic.

Don't say . . .

> I think. . .
> Can I be Frank?
> In a nutshell. . .
> In all actuality . . .
> In my own mind. . .
> Can I be honest?
> What are your needs.
> I was in the area and . . .
> We're the best in the business . . .
> Is price important to you?
> Are you the decision maker?
> What do you think?
> When will you make a decision?
> Have you looked at the information I sent you?
> We are very price competitive.
> I see your point, but . . .
> What time would be good for you?
> When can you let me know?
> How soon do you need it?
> I know you're busy, so I won't take up much of your
> time.
> Are there any other problems I can help you with?
> Can I call you in two weeks?
> Are you having any problems with . . .
> Can I help you?
> I don't know.
> We can't do that

Hang on a minute
It's our company policy to . . .
What do I have to do to earn your business?
What do you have for me today?
So, what do you think?
You'll have to . . .
Just one more thing and I'll let you go.
I was wondering . . .

What makes these phrases so pathetic is how often they're used in daily selling situations. They are not inherently bad. They are simply bland and boring. They lack originality, imagination, and are spoken without the benefit of thought and preparation. If these phrases sound familiar, maybe it's time for a verbal tune-up.

Here are a few of them. Why would you say, "I think"? Politicians are masters of answering interview questions using "I think" several times in one sentence.

When a customer asks you a question, avoid saying "I think." Say, "I feel," "I believe." For example, "I believe this application would work best for you in this situation" or "I believe this product would work in this application."

Some of these phrases are so worn out or senseless, that the listener is giving a mental response. Whenever I hear someone use the phrase "in my own mind," I think to myself – as opposed to whose mind?

"Can I be Frank?" Only if I can be Louise.

"To be honest with you . . ." Does that mean that so far you've been dishonest with me?

Here's one of my favorites. A salesperson is listening to a customer and at the right moment, he chimes in and says, "Yes, I agree," and then says "but." If you say "but," make no mistake about it, you are not agreeing. When you say "but," it signals that you are about to argue a point. It may say it in a soft way, but it still signals a different point of view not an agreement.

Many times when I'm giving a seminar, a person will raise his hand and say, "Well, Jim, that's a good point, but . . . ." And I say to myself "here it comes." What the salesperson does is proceed to tell me why he disagrees with me.

When I ask what words can be used in place of "but," the response is often "however." I like to point out that "however" is really a "but" with a bow tie. It's still not something you want to use. The correct word is "and." "That's a good point, Mr. Customer, **and** something else for you to consider is . . . ."

Tape one of your telephone sales calls with a small tape recorder. When you finish your calls listen to your words. Is your speech laced with pathetic sounding phrases? Are you bored listening to yourself? If the answer is "yes," spend more time on crafting your words.

9. It's Not An Adventure

In the game of golf, your ability is measured by a calculated handicap. The lower your handicap, the better your game is going to be.

In my sales training seminars, I often ask for a volunteer. The volunteer has to meet one criterion. He or she must have an average score in the nineties for eighteen holes of golf. A person shooting in the nineties is considered to be a high handicapper or an average golfer.

I ask the volunteer to step forward and to face the group. Next, I tell the volunteer that I'm going to ask him to take three imaginary golf shots. His instructions are to address the imagined ball and take a swing based on the situation described.

For the first shot, I ask my volunteer to imagine he is on the first tee hitting a driver. I ask him to address the ball and take his normal driver swing. Next, I ask him to imagine he's on a long, par five hole and seventy yards from the pin. Once again, I ask him to address the ball and take his regular swing with the wedge. Finally, I'll ask him to imagine he's on the seventh hole only ten yards from the green. Once again, I'll ask him to pick his club, and take his swing.

After three imaginary swings, I'll ask for a round of applause and ask him to be seated. It never fails – each time I ask a high handicapper to swing a club – he does it with confidence and without hesitation.

After the demonstration, I ask the volunteer if he has ever played professional golf or earned a great deal of money playing the game. The response is always the same, "Of course not."

Let's review what's happened. An average golfer, without hesitation, without a golf club, without a golf ball, and without grass will enthusiastically demonstrate the art of golf in front of all his peers and managers.

Then, I ask for another volunteer. I ask for a person who would be willing to demonstrate, in front of his entire organization, how to make a telephone appointment, approach a prospect, use open-ended questions, handle price objections, and finally how to ask for the order.

It's amazing – I never get any volunteers. Wonder why? It's difficult to demonstrate something you haven't practiced and for which you have no routine.

Even the average golfer, who isn't being paid for what he does, has a backpack of skills. As he approaches each shot, he knows which club he will select, how he will address the ball, and how he will adjust his swing arc and the club speed. He has practiced a variety of shots, and has established a routine that gives him confidence. More than likely, he has spent some time at the driving range before today's game to "warm up" before hitting the first ball down the middle of the fairway.

Even more importantly, as he plays the round, he will engage in a process of self-evaluation and self-analysis. He will decide what worked and what didn't, and make changes as he approaches his next shots. He mentally sees each shot as a way to improve upon a previous shot. If he misses a shot, he evaluates what he did wrong – stood too far from the ball, picked up his head, didn't account for the wind.

If the average golfer is practicing at the driving range before his game, what do you think you should be doing before your next sales call? It's insanity for you to warm-up in front of your customers.

Here is a brief list of things professional sales reps should prepare before making a sales call:

✓ Prepare written sales call objectives.

✓ Prepare your opening statement.

✓ Prepare your open-ended questions.

✓ Prepare how you will introduce benefits.

✓ Prepare your responses to common objections.

✓ Prepare the transition to your close.

✓ Prepare how you will specifically ask for the customer's commitment.

45

- ✓ Prepare how you'll secure the next appointment if you need one.

- ✓ Prepare how you will ask for referrals.

Let's define how I'm using the word "prepare." "Prepare" means to <u>think and write</u> about what you'll soon be doing in front of the customer. A lot of training programs try to get salespeople to use the same lines and responses to specific customer situations. It's only natural that you don't want to come across sounding plastic and insincere.

Typically the salespeople I've observed tend not to prepare their comments and questions in advance - instead they treat every call like an adventure.

For no particular reason and without any rationale, salespeople are reluctant to prepare and practice the specific words they use in recurring situations. Most prefer to act with random spontaneity. If you want your words to be crisp, concise, and have the maximum impact on your prospect, never wait until you're with your prospect to prepare what you're going to say.

Treating every call as an adventure is out. What's in is preparing and practicing for each critical element of the sales call. Confucius once said, "In all things, success depends upon previous preparation, and without such preparation, there is failure." Build your success on a foundation that's based on careful preparation and routine practice.

There is a huge difference between sounding canned and being prepared. Huge!

10. Four Ways to Listen Better

How's your sales presentation? Do you believe it's really good? It may not be as good as you think it is. A presentation is something that is delivered over and over again. It doesn't change from one customer to the next. That's why it's often called "a pitch." Professional salespeople don't "pitch," they present tailored solutions to very specific customer problems. In order to present the solutions, the salesperson has to diagnose the problem. The problem is diagnosed by listening to the customer. Here are four ways to sharpen your listening skills.

1. **Ask Questions** - The preeminent way to identify customer problems is to ask questions. The best questions are open-ended. They get people to open up about specific topics. You can dramatically increase your probability for success whenever you identify specific and unique customer requirements. Customers and prospects use words to describe their problems. Ideally, whenever you can relate your product or service to the customer's specific needs the solution will be more appealing to your customer.

Just like customers who use words to relate problems and needs, salespeople also use words to offer solutions in the form of products and services. The common denominator is words, the essence of verbal communications. A sales "pitch" generally uses the same words over and over like a dog and pony show. A tailored presentation adopts more appropriate words, to offer customer-specific solutions. Let me illustrate the point.

When I'm the customer, I define service as "On time, every time, and you fix it if it's broken." What if you asked a customer about his priorities and he replied service was a top priority. If you go no further, how will you define "service"? You would paraphrase using your own words, which may not match the customer's definition.

Suppose you asked the customer to define service for you. He replies, "Service is what I want, when I want it and how I want it delivered." When you begin to describe the service element for your product, how will you do it? A rep relying on his standard "pitch" will respond with his standard comment about service.

2. **Take Notes** - The professional sales representative listens actively by taking notes. He was listening. He was even taking notes. He captured the customer's definition of service

as soon as he said it. He even put it in quotes. He captured the important words used by the customer. He wants to relate to the customer, and he knows he has a better chance to connect if he relates to the customer's definition of service by using the customer's key words.

In the February 18, 2001 *Sarasota Herald Tribune*, writer David Grimes, had an article called "Bring back the waiters who write it down." He described the impact on customers when waiters don't write the order down on paper. He said, "The omission of the pad and pencil has the reverse effect on diners. The first thing that crosses their minds is: the waiter is going to screw up our order because he's not writing it down." People are flattered when you take notes. It makes them feel they said something worthy enough for your notes. If it works in restaurants, it'll work during your sales call.

3. **Take Time To Respond** - Many of you are so busy thinking about what you are going to say next, you fail to score listening points. Too often, when customers ask questions, you respond too quickly, giving the impression, you are giving your response little or no thought. Whenever your customer asks a really good question, pause five seconds to consider your response. Two things will happen. First, your response will be more professional. Second, you send the right message to the customer

when you take a moment to think before you speak.

4. **Put Quotes In Your Notes** - Let me give you an example. I was doing some research for an organization I was scheduled to speak to. I was preparing to speak to 250 dental lab owners, managers, salespeople and technicians. When you go to a dentist and he takes an impression of a tooth for a cap or crown, the dentist then sends that impression to the dental lab for the finished product.

    It so happened that about a month before this presentation I was getting a permanent crown put into my mouth. And so, while I was under Novocain I interviewed my dentist in an attempt to do some primary research. One of the questions I asked him was: "What are your priorities for your dental practice?" The dentist blinked, hesitated two seconds and said, "My top priority is to provide exceptional dentistry."

    A month later during my presentation I told the group, about 250 people in the room, about my interview with the dentist. And I asked them, "How do you think the dentist responded when I asked him the question, "What are your priorities for your dental practice?" Would you write it down? And they did. It took about thirty seconds. I asked a few people what they wrote. I got a few varied responses, and then one person said "patient care." Many of the group agreed with this response. A show of hands indicated that over 60% seemed to think "patient care" was the right answer. And then I said this, "The correct answer to my questions is this: you couldn't have known unless you were there to hear his response."

None guessed correctly because "listening" is not a guessing game. My dentist did not say "patient care." He said "exceptional dentistry." That's an example of what you'd want to put in quotes. Imagine if your product was a $15,000 intra-oral camera, and you're at a critical point during your presentation, after you've asked all of your questions. You've identified problems, needs and opportunities. You're making the presentation, trying to connect to that dentist's specific requirements. And then you say, "doctor, this camera is designed to help you provide the exceptional dentistry" that is your number one priority for your practice." Can you imagine the doctor's response? There's a connection there. But you can only work these key phrases into your presentation if you've captured them in quotes.

Taking notes is a necessity. Putting quotes in your notes, makes it even better, and will significantly raise the bar in your attempt to connect with your customer.

Make quote-taking a part of your note taking.

Remember, if you listen to their words, they will buy more from you.

Food For Thought

If listening to another person is an art, become an artist.
                                             Anonymous

Rowing harder doesn't help if the boat is headed in the wrong direction.
                                        Kenichi Ohmae

Lower your voice and people will strain to listen.
                                        George Patton

The most important thing in communication is to hear what isn't being said.
                                        Peter Drucker

11. Eliminate Watch Watchers

During a presentation, usually when you're speaking, have you ever caught a potential customer trying to sneak a peak at his watch? Of course, you have, and so have I, up until I made a discovery. What I learned was that potential customers looked at their watches when I was talking, not when they were talking. They always become more interested in any subject when they are the ones doing the talking.

And the more they talk, the less likely they'll be to look at their watches. And as a matter of fact, I've never seen a potential or actual customer look at their watches when they were talking.

Another reason to get your customers talking is that if they're spending less time looking at their watches, you'll get more quality time with them.

If you want more quality time with your prospects and customers always ask really good open-ended questions. The better the question, the more you'll learn about the person you're talking to.

Watches tell time. They don't determine how much of it a customer will give you. Getting more time depends less on what you say and more about the questions you ask.

Food For Thought

Talking is a disease of age.
> *Ben Johnson*

We talk little, if we do not talk about ourselves.
> *William Hazlitt*

The four-letter word for psychotherapy is talk.
> *Eric Hodgins*

It isn't that they can't see the solution. It is that they can't see the problem.
> *G.K. Chesterton*

Beware the fury of a patient man.
> *John Dryden*

12. Ask

In his book, *Winning With The Power Of Persuasion*, Joseph Mancuso indicated the most powerful three-letter word is the word "ask." He also said that most children ask about sixty questions a day. After they graduate from college, they're asking two questions a day and one of them is "When do we eat?" His words got me thinking.

I remember being a teenager. The two things I feared the most were asking girls to dance and having to get up and speak to groups. When it came to asking girls to dance, I don't recall what I was afraid of, especially since I liked to dance. I was probably imagining that those three pimples located prominently on my chin would turn into eight even bigger ones.

If only I could do it all over again. I realize I can't. But if only I could, here's what I'd do. Being a teenager about thirteen or fourteen, I still wouldn't be driving a car but I would have a bike. I would get on that bike and ride and practice, ride and practice. I would practice exactly what I would to say to the girl I wanted to dance with. I'd say it out loud so I could feel the words.

The night of the dance I would feel great. Actually, I'd feel like a pillar of competence and a tower of confidence. And do you know why? Of course it's because I practiced exactly what I was going to say. There would be no hesitation in my voice as I walked up to the girl I wanted to dance with and said, "I like to dance fast and I like to dance slow, which do you prefer?"

When I use this story in seminars, I like to remind people that when I was a kid, I thought the fear of rejection made me nervous. When I reflect back to those days as a young boy, I now realize what really created the anxiety for me was that I didn't know specifically how I was going to ask the girls to dance. If only I had prepared and practiced more.

Preparing questions in advance and preparing how to ask for the business are two essential core skills of the selling process that should never be left to chance and improvisation. Never!

If I knew then what I know now – I'd be the "King of Dance," at least at the West Babylon High School, my alma mater.

Ask is more than a three-letter word. Four years ago, I saw an article in *The Competitive Advantage Newsletter* with the headline – "The Most Powerful Three-Letter Word." You guessed it; the word was "ask." In sales the principal tool we use to help customers buy our products is words. Words are our tools. We live and die by them. Sales are won and lost by the proper and improper arrangement of words. When you ask really good questions, not the shoot from the lip variety, you show interest. There's no easier way to learn more about your prospects. Many salespeople recognize the value of good questions, but fail to ask them, because they neglect to prepare them. One of the biggest roadblocks to developing customers and prospects is our own mouth and what comes out of it. Instead of spending time "telling," start investing more time "asking." <u>Employ your ears before you engage your mouth.</u>

Here's what you can ask for:

Ask for the gatekeeper's help.

Ask for the appointment.

Ask for directions.

Ask for the names of the decision-makers.

Ask for an organizational chart.

Ask really good open-ended questions.

Ask for a tour of the facility.

Ask for a demonstration.

Ask for the next appointment.

Ask for a trial order.

Ask for the opportunity to send a proposal.

Ask your customers to visit your home office.

Ask your potential customers for a commitment.

Ask your customers for an extended contract.

Ask your customers for internal and external referrals.

Ask all customers for testimonial letters.

Ask your new customers for more business.

Ask your new customers for even more business.

If you don't ask, you won't receive. The more you ask, the more you'll enjoy selling.

When salespeople hesitate to ask, they do so because they have anxiety, lack confidence, and haven't prepared (word for word) what they will say in these situations. The time to prepare is definitely not when you're in front of the customer.

When you combine preparation with practice (out loud) you're on your way to achieving better results. The anxiety is gone, confidence is boosted, and your customer is more likely to respond more favorably to your professional approach.

ASKING more will help you achieve more. Preparing what you ask and practicing how you ask will give you superior results.

Go out and buy a tape recorder. Keep it on *record* as you practice what you have already prepared. At first it may seem awkward. You must replay it to hear the results. You shouldn't deprive yourself of hearing what your customers hear on a daily basis.

By eliminating mushy sales babble from your selling routine you will inevitably sound better and achieve greater results.

Buying and using a tape recorder says something about you. So does your reluctance to try something different.

Food For Thought

As is our confidence, so is our capacity.
William Hazlitt

Audacity augments courage; hesitation, fear.
Publilius Syrus

Ask, and it shall be given you; seek, and ye shall find; knock, and it shall be opened unto you.
Mathew 7:7

How forcible are right words!

Job

Words, when well chosen, have so great a force in them that a description often gives us more lively ideas than the sight of things themselves.

Joseph Addison

All words are pegs to hang ideas on.

Henry Beecher

You can stroke people with words.

F. Scott Fitzgerald

Words are the small change of thought.

Jules Renard

13. Stay Away from Basic Instincts

Let's review our basic instincts. I'm referring to the basic instincts of professional salespeople, especially the ones that guide us through our daily challenges of selling. You see; these instincts are so basic they may actually create problems that could be avoided.

Be wary of basic instincts.

Talking vs. Listening
This is a big one. Most business surveys indicate salespeople talk too much. It's because we're great communicators. We get hired because of our communication skills. When our minds become full of product information, we feel the need to vent. Usually it's right in front of a prospect or customer. Talking is easy; listening is not, especially for good communicators. Taking good notes will dramatically improve your listening skills. Remember, if you listen to their words, they will buy more from you. If you really listen to their words, they will buy even more from you.

Defending vs. Explaining
This is both common and obvious. When you expect your customers to bring up price, you are naturally ready to discuss it. We usually become so preoccupied with pricing

issues, it often detracts from developing the relevant value of the product and how it is specifically tailored to the customer's needs. Tom Winninger, in his book Price Wars, says our options are clear: "We can defend our price or we can explain our value." Remember, the former comes naturally, and the latter requires doing your homework. Also remember, if your product is better it's supposed to cost more.

Features vs. Benefits
Since so many salespeople want to present the features in considerable detail, it must be instinctive. Why else would you do it so often? The facts are easy to discuss because they are so evident. Product features are listed in detailed sheets, are focused on ad nauseam during sales training sessions, and are easily recited during a sales call. Benefits, however, must be presented in a way in which they relate to your customer's specific requirements. Benefits create interest by being a significant part of the value chain. Features are logical and benefits are emotional. If you want to become more passionate about your products, don't miss the opportunity to show how each prospect or customer benefits from using your product. Present your benefits in an enthusiastic way, and they'll get a better reception. The focus should always be on how your customers will gain from using your products.

Winging It vs. Singing It
The single most important tool a salesperson possesses is his words. There are only twenty-six letters in the alphabet and so many words to choose from, we usually give in to our instincts and confidence to wing our questions and more disturbingly, wing our most common responses to

recurring objections. What begins as a comment or response ends up as sales babble. It turns into babble because whenever we don't know exactly what we're going to say, we always end up saying more than we intended. The best song begins as a selection of words on sheet music. Did you ever wonder how a singer makes a song come alive? The singer studies the words with the music, and then begins singing by matching the words to the rhythm and tempo of the song. Don't wing it; sing it. Make sure your words match your music. Even better, make sure your words relate to your buyer's specific needs.

Mental Notes vs. Written Notes
Our basic instinct is to remember important information by making mental notes. The problem with mental notes is that they aren't always retrievable on demand. How many, "I just remembered I was supposed to . . ." come too late. The sales rep who says "I keep everything in my head" is fooling himself into thinking he has good notes. As information doubles every year and our anxiety levels loom larger, your head is probably the worst place to keep important information. Listen carefully to what your customers say and always take good notes. Not only does your note taking show your interest, you'll be better prepared for the next sales call.

I continue to be amazed in restaurants where the trend seems to be for the waiters or waitresses to take the order and not write anything down. Recently at a very pricey hotel, I inquired about the fish of the day (grouper), but I ordered roasted chicken. The waiter, who failed to write down my order, brought me the grouper. This is not a rare occurrence. I'm sure you have encountered the same situation. Without notes, the waiter either returns to ask, "What did you want?" or brings something you did not order.

Thirty years ago when life was simpler, you could get away with making mental notes about your prospects and customers. Today, everything is more complicated. Neglecting good notes sends the signal that you don't care. If you care, take notes. If you care a lot, make sure you capture your customers' key words in quotes. Today's street-smart salespeople include "customer quotes" in their notes – do you?

Improvising vs. Preparing

Which is easier to do, improvise or prepare? Naturally, improvising takes less effort. Let's stand in the customer's shoes for a moment. Do you think the customer can distinguish preparation from improvisation? Of course he can. Preparation isn't an accident. Preparation reveals character. A lack of preparation is also revealing. Prepared salespeople demonstrate professionalism. Professional salespeople always earn more money than mediocre ones.

Henry Ford said, "Before everything else, getting ready is the secret of success." It was true then and it's even more important today. The path to professionalism begins with preparation. What should you prepare? Everything!

Starting tomorrow what are you currently improvising that would sound better with more preparation and practice? If you're delighted with your results and current income – there's no need to make changes. On the other hand, if you want better results and a higher personal income for yourself make change a daily habit.

Start each day by asking this question. "What's the one thing I can improve and change today that will have a positive impact on my performance and my income?" Then just do it. It sure beats procrastination and "business as usual."

Food For Thought

Man's natural instinct is never toward what is sound and true; it is toward what is specious and false.

Mencken

Too much improvisation leaves the mind stupidly void. Running beer gathers no foam.

Victor Hugo

When it comes to body language, there are some who have better vocabularies than others.

Doug Larson

A moment's insight is sometimes worth a life's experience.

O.W. Holmes

Common sense is the wick of the candle.

Emerson

A short saying contains much wisdom.

Sophocles

Do your work with your whole heart and you will succeed – there is so little competition.

Elbert Hubbard

14. The Price Is Right

You're a salesperson. You sell products. It doesn't matter what kind. Your company gives you some flexibility when it comes to price. Your price has elasticity. You have control.

Question: Which do you think of first, the most you can sell your product for or the least you can sell it for? Be honest.

When asked to justify your answer, do you feel anxious and defensive? You are defensive about your opinions, your beliefs, and your values. Most of us are extremely comfortable justifying our positions. Remember Winninger's quote from *Price Wars*: "We can explain our value or defend our price." Most of us spend too much time playing defense. I know I did it. That was then. I stopped doing it as soon as I realized I was leaving too much money on the table. Now when I leave money on the table, I take it personally.

As a professional sales trainer, it's not easy for me to admit. I am just as gun-shy about price as you are. Let me give you a real-life example.

Six years ago I had a phone call from the president of a small, medical supply company. He told me he had five salespeople and an inside customer service person. He was very interested in providing sales training for this small team of his. Two months earlier, I had just raised my fees 20%.

The first thought I had after he told me about the size of his organization, was that there was no way I could charge him my new fee. I took my new fee and entered it into my desktop calculator and proceeded to divide it by the number of sales reps he had. I caught myself talking myself out of a more profitable sale.

Well, I couldn't control having that thought, <u>but I could exercise control over how I reacted to it</u>. So, I began asking open-ended questions. I asked him to describe his sales organization. He did in considerable detail. I asked him about previous sales training, and he mentioned there hadn't been any previous training. He reminded me that we had talked three years earlier when he was a sales manager and worked for his father. His father was retired; and he was now President.

I asked him what made him decide to call me back after three years. He told me about his company's success and his desire to keep the momentum going. Everything about his business was changing – markets, customers, products, competition, and of course the federal government's involvement or meddling with health care. Given all the changes, he viewed sales training not as an option but as a necessity.

A funny thing happened while I was listening to his responses to my questions. He convinced me, yes – he convinced me, to present my new and higher fee. I really wanted to thank him. He'll never know how close I came to giving him a whopping discount two minutes into the telephone call.

That's the story and here's the point. Actually there are two points. First, never give into your negative thoughts especially when they relate to price. Second, never offer a price until you have completed a comprehensive assessment of your prospect's needs. By not jumping the gun, you can avoid giving a discount that isn't necessary.

New Customers
Encourage your customers to tell you their story before you tell yours. And remember; never give a price before you get their complete story. The price is right when your product matches their needs and when your value exceeds their requirements and expectations.

Also, eliminate the words "price" and "cost." Use the word "investment." Most products can be positioned as "investments."

Try going an entire day without using the words "price" and "cost." It won't be easy, but it will be more profitable for you.

Food For Thought

All good things are cheap: all bad things are expensive.

Thoreau

Its only expensive is you
don't use it,

The real price of everything is the toil and trouble of acquiring it.

Adam Smith

Those things are dearest to us that have cost us the most.

Montaigne

We never know the true worth of water until the well is dry.

Thomas Fuller

That which cost little is less valued.

Cervantes

Nothing is intrinsically valuable; the value of everything is attributed to it, assigned to it from outside the thing itself, by people.

John Barth

Part III

Questions

15. Over-Used Questions

The most frequently asked questions are "Can I help you?" and "Is everything okay?" Every day, this ritual is repeated. In every city in our great country you can walk into most department stores and expect to be greeted with the all too familiar, "Can I help you?" Have you ever wondered why this is so commonplace? Well I have, and it occurred to me that people say this because they don't know what else to say. They haven't been trained to say anything else, and they have heard others use this phrase so they repeat it.

In restaurant after restaurant, usually as you're putting food into your mouth, you can anticipate the server asking you, "Is everything okay?" A thumb's up or a nod of the head is usually taken as an affirmative reply.

The questions are so routine that many times the answers are ignored. As I was paying a restaurant bill, the cashier asked:"Was everything okay?" I said: "The service was rather slow; the soup was cold when it was served; and I never did get my second cup of coffee." The cashier smiled and said: "Oh sorry, that will be $10.42."

The cashier didn't really want to know if "everything was okay," and if it wasn't okay there was nothing she was going to do to rectify matters. The question was routine and nothing more. Some manager probably told her to ask the question as customers left the restaurant. Unfortunately, the manager didn't tell her what to do when the customer did not reply, "everything was fine."

The "How are you?" questions falls into this same category. Most questioners really don't want to hear about your aches and pains or your latest surgery. The question fills up the silence void.

If you want to sound like everyone else and you want to fill the silence with useless questions, then ask away. You will get useless replies.

If you want to use your questions to sell more, then you have more to learn about questions.

Asking questions is the essence of selling. Why is it then, so few salespeople can demonstrate their questioning skills?

Ask any professional comedian to give you eight of his best jokes and he won't blink or hesitate before he shares them enthusiastically with you.

Ask almost any sales representative to share his eight best customer questions and you're apt to see a look of anxiety on his face. Long after the comedian has told his jokes, most salespeople are still trying to recall the questions they have asked.

There's only one reason why a comedian can share his eight best jokes and a sales person cannot share his eight best questions.

The comedian knows his jokes like the back of his hand. Therefore there's no thinking and no blinking.

Do you know your best questions?

Food For Thought

A question not to be asked is a question not to be answered.
          Robert Southey: The Doctor XII

I keep six honest serving-men
(they taught me all I knew):
Their names are What and Why and When
And How and Where and Who
          Rudyard Kipling: The Serving-men

The most difficult thing in the world is to say thinkingly what everybody says without thinking.

Alain

A fool uttereth all his mind.

Bible

You can stroke people with words.
F. Scott Fitzgerald

Nothing is so firmly believed, as what we least know.

Montaigne

From listening comes wisdom, and from speaking repentance.

Italian Proverb

His answer trickled through my head,
Like water through a sieve.

Lewis Carrol:
Through the Looking-Glass VIII

16. Characteristics Of Great Questions

Questions that seek information all share some common characteristics. As you work to develop your questions make sure you make the transition from mind to paper. If it's not in writing, you can't make it better. David Frost once said, "You can judge the quality of the question by the quality of the response." If you want to sound confident, prepare your questions in writing and make sure they have the following characteristics.

- **Brevity** – Less is more. Create questions that have no more than ten words. Certainly you'll find exceptions to this rule. But if you want to be clear, you must be concise. Short and sweet, is better than long and sour. As you begin to prepare your questions in writing, be sure you count the number of words you are using.

- **Necessity** – Every word must be a keeper. If you want to make more sales, master the language. Every word <u>must add value</u>. If the word doesn't add value and isn't needed, eliminate it from your question. A really good question is like a burning ember; it has the potential to linger on.

- **Personalized** – Your questions should include the word "you." Direct your questions to your customer. Your questions demonstrate your interest. Put your customers into your questions and they will put you into their responses.

- **Open-ended** – Make sure your questions can't be answered with one word. Remember, you're not a lawyer; you're an explorer. You won't discover much if you ask "yes" and "no" type questions. Your objective is to get the customer talking. To minimize your talking and to maximize their talking, ask deep questions that provoke thoughtful and insightful answers.

Listening to what your customers say and how they say it should be the centerpiece to every sales presentation. You don't have to fill every void with the sound of your own voice. <u>Silence is golden on a sales call</u>. Don't screw it up by talking too much. There are four primary behavioral styles. If you ask each style the same question, two will respond quickly and the other two require time to think about their answers. Don't be too quick to break the silence and interrupt their thinking.

Always be quick to listen and slow to speak.

17. The Best Twelve Questions To Ask Customers

If you want to ask really good questions, you must do three things. First, you must prepare them. Once prepared, the questions must be organized in a logical sequence. Finally, you must be sure to ask them.

The following are my favorite questions. Some aren't even stated as questions, but they work the same way – they get the customer talking. If you like them, please use them. If they don't quite fit your mouth, change them. These questions work for me, and I'm confident if you give them a try, they'll work for you.

1. Tell me about your business.

    This is a very broad question by design. Now, before you ask this question always tell the customer you've done some preliminary research. You previewed their web site, looked at their financials, and downloaded several recent articles about their company. When the customer begins to answer, what usually comes to the surface pretty quickly is what's important to the customer. If you're selling products to the government, you can substitute the word "organization" for the word "business." The beauty of a really good question is that it eliminates all assumptions. It forces you to start with your potential customer, not with your products.

2. Describe the people in your organization.

   Once again, it's a very broad question that is designed to get the potential customer talking about what's important to him. Listen carefully to his response to this one. You will be rewarded with how this person feels about and possibly relates to other key people in his organization. Another really good question to ask is: "In addition to you, who else is involved in making decisions for (name the product)?"

3. What are your responsibilities?

   Once you discover the role, title, or position within an organization, also probe to find out what a person's responsibilities are. Here's where you'll get a measure of his ego, self-esteem and self worth. Most salespeople seldom ask this question because they make goofy assumptions based on what they know about certain job titles. *In the long run, making goofy assumptions will make you goofy.* Ask the question and you'll learn more.

4. What are the biggest challenges you face in growing your business?

    This is a terrific question and the key word is "challenges." It's a positive word that uncovers negative stuff. As a professional salesperson, your job is to identify specific needs and problems. When you first meet a potential customer, it's not always easy for him to open up to a stranger about problems, regardless of your sincerity and willingness to help. To speed up the process, focus on "challenges" instead of "problems." Most people are more than willing to describe their biggest challenges even if they are reluctant to discuss their problems. Change the way you ask the question, and you'll see how they change the way they respond to you. Listen carefully to their response to this question and be sure to take good notes.

5. What are your priorities?

    This question uses only four words. It doesn't get any easier than this one and it's a gem. Here's what you'll learn. Some people don't have priorities, and this question makes those people easy to spot. If they do have priorities, they'll describe them in detail. If you get a long list, ask the customer to prioritize it for you. If on the other hand, the list is small, ask the customer if there are any additional priorities. This is an assumption buster question. If you don't ask it, you are probably making too many assumptions about your potential customers.

The response to this question paves the way for you to tailor your presentation to match the customer's priorities. Remember to take detailed notes after you ask this question.

6. Ask a relationship question.

   Email Cord
   Conn/years
   When did they graduate Dental school/years

   Of the twelve questions, this one will vary according to the situation. It's a personal question designed to learn about common interests and things that contribute over time to building a personal relationship. Often you'll notice pictures, trophies, plaques and other memorabilia that reveal personal interests. Ask any question that advances the relationship to a higher level. Make sure it's an open-ended question. "Did you catch that fish?" is the wrong question to ask if you want him to tell you about his fishing story.

7. What do you like most about your current supplier/product?

   Put your ego aside for this one. Naturally, you want to hear that he doesn't like anything about his current supplier and that's why he's agreed to speak with you. In the real world, however, he probably likes something about his present supplier. These are his hot buttons. It doesn't make a difference whether your products can deliver these hot buttons or not, you must know what they are before you begin your sales presentation.

8. If you could change anything about your current supplier/product, what would you change?

This question is an exception to the ten word maximum. I just like it this way. It's a powerful question, and if you are patient, you will be rewarded with a good response. <u>Remember this</u>; fifty percent of the time his first response will be: "I can't think of anything." Be patient and point out that nothing is perfect. Ask the question again, and wait patiently for his answer. No customer is ever 100% satisfied. What you're searching for is that dissatisfaction, no matter how small it may be. Once identified, you have a starting point on which to build your presentation. People are always looking to improve their current situation. Don't make any assumptions. This is an opportunity question.

9. What are your criteria for making a decision?

I'm absolutely amazed at how infrequently this question is asked, especially since it's one of the most powerful questions in the line-up. You'll discover if your customer even has criteria. If he does, he'll tell you what they are. Once he describes the criteria, you can ask him to prioritize them for you. When he answers this question, he is telling you what he is going to specifically base his decision on. Ask one hundred different people and you'll hear one hundred different answers. How could you begin to make an intelligent sales presentation without knowing what his decision is going to be based on? Try this one on for size and you'll get an immediate pay back. If he responds to this question by saying price or budget, use this follow-up question to set aside the pricing issue. "In addition to price, what other criteria do you have?" It really works!

10. Describe your decision making process.

The criteria and process are related yet different. You need to know what criteria will be evaluated before the decision is made. You also need to know the process involved in making the decision. What steps will the customer actually go through to reach a final decision? Basically you'll learn whether it's going to be a toss of the coin or a more complicated process. Either way, you'll be better positioned to tailor your presentation to accommodate the customer's criteria and the process he'll use to make a decision. The larger the "deal" the more important this question becomes.

11. How will you measure success when using our products?

This is one of my favorite questions. It's so revealing it's scary. You will hear things that you couldn't have imagined in your wildest dreams. That's the beauty of the question. There's no way you can accurately anticipate a response to this question. Ask the question, relax, and listen carefully to the answers you get. This question unearths the personal and critical measurements the individual has for your product. <u>Wouldn't you like to hear the answer to this one before you start to sell your products</u>? You bet!

12. What are your expectations when working with a new supplier?

This one is very straightforward. Expectations are a powerful and dominant influence. If you want to build a long-term customer relationship, ask the expectations question. If you think you already know . . . how could you possible know if you haven't asked? That's the point. It's a great question. Try it and you'll be delighted with the results.

There are so many reasons for asking really good questions and only one reason for not asking them. We don't ask really good questions if we're in a rush to make the sale. <u>This isn't about making a sale; it's about building a relationship</u>. It's about helping potential customers make more informed buying decisions. It's about professional salespeople doing their homework before selling their products. It's about getting to know your customers in order to tailor your products to their specific needs.

A good question reinforces your selling proposition.

Food For Thought

He who asks questions cannot avoid the answers.

Cameroonian Proverb

There aren't any embarrassing questions – just embarrassing answers.

Carl Rowan

To question a wise man is the beginning of wisdom.

German Proverb

Questions open doors; answers close them.

Anonymous

18. Questions Build Confidence

A while ago, I was giving a selling skills workshop. It was in Indianapolis, scheduled for a half-day. In the middle of the presentation, a man raised his hand and asked if he could make a comment. His name was John.

John told the group that he and his wife had been looking for a baby sitter. Two to three weeks went by and they couldn't find one so they placed an ad in the newspaper. A couple of teenagers called, and then a woman responded. The woman started to ask John questions over the phone. Questions like: "What are the names of your children?" "How old are they?" "What did your children like most about the baby sitters you've had in the past?" "If your children could change anything about the baby sitters you've used in the past, what would they want to change?" The woman asked a few more questions then gave a brief account of experiences. She provided references and informed John and his wife that she was CPR certified.

As John was finishing his comments, a woman in the back of the room raised her hand. "Did you hire her?" she asked. Before John answered, I asked a question of my own. I turned to John and said, "John, when the woman was asking you all those questions how did it make you feel?"

Now here's what John said, and I'll never forget it. He said, "It made me feel infinitely more confident in her."

Then I turned to the woman in the back of the room and asked her to repeat her question. "Well John, did you hire her?" And John said, "I booked her for three months."

Why do questions build confidence? How do questions create a more positive response to us? If really good questions are so powerful, why don't more salespeople ask them?

Laziness, procrastination, and an "I've always done it this way" attitude are the three major roadblocks to asking better questions. Your questions will only work if you prepare and practice them.

Good questions are seldom the result of spontaneous improvisation while you're seated in front of your customer.

Awesome questions are always the result of preparation and execution. At the end of the day you'll get the opportunity to deliver your products only if you deliver really good customer questions.

Awesome questions aren't accidents.

19. The Sales Manager's Kid

I can't resist telling you this story. My biggest client hires me four or five times a year. Usually they bring me in to conduct a three-day basic selling skills program for their new hires. Occasionally, they'll bring me in to conduct a two-day fundamental of sales management training.

Last year, I was working with a group of fifteen brand new sales managers. On the morning of the second day just before lunch, I launched into a three-minute commercial for my books and audiocassette tapes. I passed out fifteen order forms and fourteen were returned with orders to purchase products.

The order form was printed on bright goldenrod stationery. It was apparent who was the one holdout. As we broke for lunch, he approached me. He explained the reason why he wasn't buying my books and tapes today. He told me he had already purchased them off my web site over a year ago. I was relieved and flattered.

As we walked to lunch together, he told me a story. He has two sons, one in college and one in high school. Both are very interested in pursuing business careers. He gave one of my books to each son with instructions to read the book and to provide their reactions to their father. Fortunately, both enjoyed reading the books and encouraged their father to do the same.

The sales manager went on to say that his family had relocated the previous summer. The younger boy was now a senior attending a new high school. Early in the fall, the sales manager and his wife attended the school's Open House where they had the opportunity to meet their son's new teachers. Because both parents worked and because they were new to the community, the sales manager gave each teacher his business card, which of course had his telephone number, pager number, and e-mail address. He told all the teachers to use any of these numbers if they ever needed to contact him or his wife.

About two weeks later, he received a call from his son's history teacher. The teacher asked him, "What kind of work do you do?" At that time, he was in sales management and told her that. He immediately asked, "What's wrong; what's the matter?'

The history teacher replied, "I've been teaching for twenty-two years and your son did something last week that I have never experienced before. The teacher told the sales manger how his son had stayed after class one day the previous week and started asking her questions.

What qualities are you looking for in a student?

What are the biggest challenges I can expect in your class?

What should my priorities be in your class?

What are your criteria for giving out A's?

How do you measure the success of your students in your class?

What are you expectations for new transfer students?

It's obvious that the teacher was impressed with the sales manager's son because of the questions he asked.

Try asking theses questions, and you'll be amazed at the results you get and the reception you'll receive from the people you call on.

The student asked my questions and impressed the teacher. Try these questions with your customers and see for yourself what happens.

Selling is an art and these questions will make you "state of the art."

Food For Thought

Understanding   is   the   beginning   of approving.

                                        Andre Gide

Tis not every question that deserves an answer.
                                    Thomas Fuller

A teacher affects eternity; he can never tell where his influence stops.
                                    Henry Adams

A teacher is better than two books.
                                    German Proverb

As a man thinketh so is he, and as a man chooseth so is he.
                                    Ralph Waldo Emerson

A smooth sea never made a skillful mariner.
                                    English Proverb

A moment's insight is sometimes worth a life's experience.
                                    Oliver Wendell Holmes, Sr.

Part IV

Staying On Top Of Your Game

20. 15 Ways To Get Really Motivated

First, recognize that motivation is an inside job. The word motivate means to impel, inspire, hope, stimulate, incite, propel, spur, goad, move, induce, prompt, instigate, fire, provoke, actuate, cause, egg on, drive, excite, and to trigger. Don't wait for someone to motivate you, here are ways you can motivate yourself.

- Set daily, weekly, monthly, yearly and lifetime goals. A goal is a goal if it's in writing. Goals get you going in the direction that's right for you.

- Listen to a motivational tape. Record into a tape recorder your favorite quotes, anecdotes and personal success stories. Play back your tape frequently. Nothing is more motivating than the sound of your own voice. Try it!

- Get motivated to make better telephone calls by buying Art Sobczak's new book, *How To Sell More In Less Time With No Rejection*. To order call Art at 402-895-9399 or visit his web site www.businessbyphone.com.

- To overachieve every quota you are given take this advice. First write yourself a check dated for 12/31/__ (enter year) payable to yourself and write how much you want to earn on the amount line. Make three laminated copies and and put one in your briefcase, auto console, and home office. Second, always aim higher than the quota you are given. If you adjust your aim, the results will follow. This is a very powerful visual motivator.

- Buy an inspirational book of quotations and keep it in your car. Read three quotes daily. Remember - inspirational words can be a powerful motivator for you.

- Invest 15 minutes daily to read books and articles about the selling profession. This is gourmet food for your brain. Don't skip a day. A day without reading is like a day without oxygen. Don't even think about it.

- Get a mentor, preferably one outside of your company. The truly successful people in business never go it alone.

- To jack-up your sales performance, prepare your own laminated cue cards. Create cue cards for making appointments, your 12 best questions, for handling the price objection, and for asking for the order. Each cue card should be prepared word-for-word. Your performance will sky rocket.

- Buy a composition notebook for your car. Record your successes, failures, and daily observations about your selling environment.

- Read the *The Ancient Scrolls* an inspiring book by Tim Connor. To order call 800-222-9070 or e-mail him at speaker@bellsouth.net.

- To get motivated about improving your personal financial situation, set a personal net worth goal and write it on a spreadsheet, then review it monthly. <u>Self worth increases proportionately with net worth</u>.

- Tell your family if you achieve 110% or more of your annual sales quota - you'll take them anywhere they want to go on vacation.

- Tell your family that when you reach a new monthly sales record milestone you'll take them out to celebrate.

- Select one song that really gets you moving and play it every morning as you back out of your driveway.

- Make a dinner date with your spouse to have dinner together tonight, then go some place special.

Every day is a great day, especially if you don't see your name in the obituary section of the paper. When you're motivated you can make every day a masterpiece.

Jim Meisenheimer

Food For Thought

All that we do is done with an eye to something else.

Aristotle

On the neck of the young man sparkles no gem so gracious as enterprise.

Hafiz

Go and wake up your luck.

Persian Proverb

Nothing will ever be attempted, if all possible objections must first be overcome.

Samuel Johnson

None will improve your lot, if you yourselves do not.

Bertolt Brecht

21. Build "Awesome" Customer Relationships

What's the one thing starting today that you could start doing or stop doing that would have a dramatic impact on your customer relationships? It's a great question. Think about it.

It takes a great deal of effort and an extraordinary amount of energy to close "a big deal." Never forget, it may take even more effort and energy, to keep the business after you win it.

Consider the word AWESOME and all that means. To be awesome is to be formidable, imposing, grand, impressive, outstanding, wonderful, excellent, and even remarkable.

- **A - Ask** good customer questions

  The two types of questions salespeople ask are open and closed. Let's raise the bar on that thinking. Questions can be open and closed and they can also be wide and deep. The wide questions are surface questions i.e. "How's it going, how's business," and "Are there any other any problems I can help you with?" A deep question always leaves its mark i.e. "What would have to happen for me to be the best distributor you ever worked with?" David Frost, the famous interviewer, once said "you can tell the quality of a question by the quality of the response." Are you asking quality questions?

- **W - Work** your priorities and prioritize your work

Prioritizing will make you enterprising. To be really effective you must be able to distinguish between what is urgent and what is important. Be careful not to start the very fires you're trying to put out. For example, eliminate the following from your voice mail message, "if it's really important page me or call me on my cell phone." The only people who don't possess a FedEx mentality are the people who work for FedEx. Everybody else thinks everything else is always a high priority. Develop the habit of sticking to your priorities. Be like a postage stamp – stick to it until you get it done.

- **E - Energize** yourself every day with a positive attitude

People with positive attitudes live longer, enjoy life more, and tend to be more likable, from their customer's perspective. I learned a long time ago, we either affect or infect the people we meet every day. Don't bring your personal problems to work because they never add value to your customers. Remember, your customer's have their own problems, so there's no need to burden them with yours. People with positive attitudes are enthusiastic, animated, excited, smiling, and always expect the best things to happen. "Your face is your own fault after age forty," according to Cicero, so check it often with a mirror.

- **S - Style** is important

  If you agree, you must be a chameleon. Most strained customer relationships are created by different styles. There is the "Driver" who is very assertive, demanding and autocratic. There is also the "Expressive" who is extremely sociable, loves to talk, and lousy with details. Then there is the "Analytical" who is very precise, organized, and extremely neat. Finally, there is the "Amiable" who is generally low-key, trusting, and very innovative. The biggest key to improving customer relationships is the art of adapting your selling style to your customers' buying style.

- **O - Others-focused**

  Another ingredient to a successful sales career is the ability to build relationships while taking care of business. Here are several ideas: don't make people feel invisible, always maintain good eye contact, remember, you can't smile enough on the telephone or in person, watch your body language, only do dog and pony shows if your customer needs a dog and pony, and add the words "for you" to the end of your sentences.

- **M - Master** the business basics

  Listen to your voice mail message. If it doesn't sound upbeat, enthusiastic and professional change it. When using E-mail, use creative subject lines and remember less is more if you want your message to be crisp and clear. Form the habit of writing personal handwritten notes using a fountain pen. It's a great way to be a "high-touch" person in the "high-tech" world we live in today.

- **E - Enthusiasm**

  Some people walk into a room and light it up. Other people walk into the same room and cast a giant shadow. Get excited about your work. If you don't like it, change it. Your life is too important and too short to waste it doing something your not passionate about.

Being AWESOME is no small task, especially when the customer is doing the evaluation. If you strive to be effective be attentive to your customers' needs, and you too can be AWESOME.

When was the last time someone called you AWESOME? If it's been a while, it may be time for some changes.

22. Keep Your Selling Skills Sharpened

Like a chef's knife or a gardener's shears that need to be sharpened periodically; so do your selling skills. Don't rely on your company to provide all of the training. There is much you can do on your own to improve your performance.

- Read selling skills stuff for a minimum of fifteen minutes every day. Read anything that will improve your selling effectiveness. I strongly recommend "Selling Power Magazine." You can sign up for their free Selling Power newsletter at selling power.com.

- Commit to buying and reading one personal /professional development book every month. I recommend *Patton On Leadership - strategic lessons for corporate warfare.* It's an excellent book and easy to read.

- Commit to buying and listening to one audio-cassette tape every week. You can turn your car into a classroom and turn windshield time into quality learning time.

- Start a reading file and load it with professional development articles. Buy one dozen manila folders and label them with the following topics: time management, prospecting, telephone skills, questioning skills, presentation skills, handling objections, value added selling, negotiating, closing, territory management, sales force automation, and communication skills.

- Start a support group or join an existing one. Don't be a lone ranger sales rep. Hangout with salespeople who share your challenges and personal values. You will be amazed how this can add to your self-esteem and boost your self-confidence. This will have a tremendously positive impact on your business.

- Join a Toastmaster's group to hone your speaking and presentation skills. To be really effective in today's global marketplace you must acquire the skills to make every standup presentation standout.

- Add up how much you spend for haircuts each year and commit to invest twice as much for personal development program /seminars. Don't wait and don't expect your company to be 100 percent responsible for your professional development.

- Keep a journal (composition notebook) of all good ideas, techniques, quotes that inspire you.

Instead of putting you're ideas and notes on Post-it notes, record them in a notebook.

- Prepare in writing the critical components to the selling process. List all the steps you typically take to make a sale. Identify all the skills required for each step. Identify your shortcomings and <u>immerse</u> yourself in them to convert them into strengths.

- Practice into a tape recorder what you prepared. Never wing these selling skills: making appointments, your best questions, recurring objections, closing the sale, and getting referrals. Once you prepare the above practice saying them into a tape recorder. Not only will your confidence increase, your sales will increase dramatically.

- Practice into a video camera if you want to really raise the bar. Record a five to ten minute product presentation. First, replay the video without the audio. Focus on your body language. Second, replay the video and turnaround so you can focus on what you said and how you said it. Third, play it again watching and listening for improvement opportunities.

- Visit one or both of these web sites weekly - salesdoctors.com and justsell.com. These are dedicated web sites for sales professionals.

- Read *Investor's Business Daily* – especially the "Leaders and Success" page. It's the single best page in any U.S. daily newspaper.

Keep fine-tuning your skills. You will be generously rewarded for your effort.

Dull saws don't cut as much wood as sharpened ones. Dull selling skills won't generate, as much sales as sharpened selling skills will.

Food For Thought

Man is not the sum of what he has already, but rather the sum of what he does not yet have, of what he could have.

Jean-Paul Sartre

If you're bored with life – you don't get up every morning with a burning desire to do things – you don't have enough goals.

Lou Holtz

All things are possible until they are proved impossible – and even the impossible may only be so, as of now.

Pearl S. Buck

23. Improvement Is A Continuous Process

Have you ever been frustrated with your skill level and results when playing a sport? The typical golfer, I guess fit that category, he plays too little and practices even less and still becomes very frustrated when that little white ball decides to go off in its own direction.

I'm just back from a week in Florida. It was great. The weather was picture perfect and I even enjoyed several rounds of golf. Between reading golf magazines and watching him play golf on TV, I've become a big fan of Tiger Woods. He's truly incredible.

I always imagined that he is just simply gifted with a great golf swing and love for the game.

Now, I'm not so sure. *Investor's Business Daily* did a profile on him. Here's some new information about this twenty-five year old phenomenal golfer.

> **Fact:** By the time, he was six he was scoring in the 90's on regulation golf courses. **Lesson:** He's been at this for nineteen years.

Fact: As a six year old, his father Earl bought him motivational tapes to listen to. **Lesson:** He's been filling his head with positive thoughts for nineteen years. How many salespeople at any age could say they've listened to motivational tapes for eighteen years?

Fact: As a six year old, he would practice swinging his golf clubs in front of a mirror while listening to these inspirational tapes. **Lesson:** Sure, he's been playing the game for eighteen years. He's also been practicing everything about the game for the same amount of time.

Fact: He wrote down many of the key messages from these tapes and posted them on his bedroom walls. They included "I smile at obstacles," "My will moves mountains," and "I do it with all my heart." **Lesson:** Our personal habits have a tremendous influence over our accomplishments. What do you have taped on your walls?

Fact: Since September 1996 he has won eighteen tournaments. This includes four majors. His career earnings of $17.4 million lead the tour. He spends hours practicing on his days off and during tournaments. He lifts weights and jogs routinely to improve his physical conditioning. **Lesson:** It takes dedication, hard work, focus, and constant improvement to achieve what Tiger Woods has achieved.

Tiger Woods makes it look so easy when he wins. That's what I see. What I never appreciated before now is how much sweat equity he puts into his work. His success is no accident.

Success is never an accident. Let's get to work. There's much to do.

- As a professional salesperson, what can you do better?

- What habits can you change?

      1.

      2.

      3.

- Which presentation can you rehearse in front of a mirror? Which tapes can you listen to on a daily basis to fill your head with positive thoughts?

      1.

      2.

- How much physical exercise can you build into your daily routine?

- How much more sweat equity can you put into your selling effort?

Make everyday a better one; by committing to continuous and gradual improvement.

Food For Thought

If you can dream it, you can do it.
                              Walt Disney

The man who is swimming against the stream knows the strength of it.
                              Woodrow Wilson

People see opportunity pointing right at them, and only one in thousands will take advantage of it.
                              Everett Greenbaum

No one can make you feel inferior without your consent.
                              Eleanor Roosevelt

Competition doesn't create character it reveals it.
                              Anonymous

24. A Son Teaches His Father A Lesson

The father shared this lesson with me, and I want to share it with you. Alfred Saldana, Jr. shared this with me during his company's sales training program. His son's name is Trey Saldana.

"My son Trey played football since the 7th grade and never scored a touchdown. In his freshman year he was moved to the fullback position and really came close several times during the season, but always came up a little short. In the morning of his last game, as I was driving him to school, he had a far away look in his eyes and I asked him if anything was wrong?"

"He said, 'Dad, today I feel this is going to be my day to score that touchdown because it's been so long.' During the last five minutes of the game he made a great run but was tackled on the eight-yard line."

"As they lined up for a pass play that was called, Trey came out of the backfield to catch the ball on the five-yard line fighting his way to the end zone and scoring his first ever touchdown."

"At dinner, after the game, Trey said, 'Dad, I told you that this was going to be my day and I did it. My goal was to score that touchdown. When I got the ball on the five-yard line my focus was to cross that goal line no matter what was in front of me because that was my goal and no one was going to take it away from me.' After dinner I went to my office to do some work and suddenly I realized my son had just taught me an invaluable lesson – no goals are impossible when you focus on the goal and just make it happen. I went back to his room and hugged him and thanked him for the lesson he just taught me."

That's Alfred's story and here's a take-a-way for you.

Impossible dreams become possible when they become goals.

Your goals must be in writing.

Your goals must be specific and measurable.

Your goals must have completion dates.

Food For Thought

> *Where much is expected from an individual, he may rise to the level of events and make the dream come true.*
> *Elbert Hubbard*

FAX Order Form 941-907-0441

Item	Price	No.	Total

Books

47 Ways to Sell Smarter — $19.95

50 More Ways To Sell Smarter — $19.95

How To Double Your Sales
Without Quadrupling Your Effort — $19.95

The Twelve Best Questions To Ask Customers — $19.95

57 Ways To Take Control Of Your Time And Your Life — $24.95

Special recordings

CD – Closing The Sale — $57.00

CD - How To Sell Anything For List Price — $57.00

CD – 35 Ways To Differentiate Yourself — $57.00

CD – Album – Surefire Selling Results — $99.00

CD – Album – 57 Ways To Take Control Of
Your Time and Your Life — $99.00

Sales Manual

No-Brainer Ways To Beat Your Competition
At The Pricing Game — $39.95

Subtotal

Tax (FL residents add 6.5%)

Shipping & handling: $5/ CD, $5/book, $7.50/album

TOTAL

Please call for special value pricing when ordering large quantities.

Method of Payment: Check or money order payable to Jim Meisenheimer, Inc:

Credit Card: ❑ Visa ❑ Master Card ❑ Amex

No:_____ Exp. Date:_____

Name:_____ Company_____

Street Address_____ City/State/Zip_____

Phone_____ FAX_____ E-mail_____

Jim Meisenheimer

About the Author

Jim Meisenheimer is the creator of No-Brainer Sales Training. His sales techniques and selling skills focus on practical ideas that get immediate results. You can discover all his secrets by contacting him at (800) 266-1268, e-mail: jim@meisenheimer.com or by visiting his website: http://www.meisenheimer.com

Jim Meisenheimer was born in New York City and was raised in West Babylon Long Island. He graduated from the University of Rhode Island and did graduate work at St. Johns University.

He is a former U.S. army officer serving in Germany and was a Public Information Officer on a General's Staff while serving in Vietnam. He was also **Vice President of Sales and Marketing for the Scientific Products Division of Baxter International**.

First and foremost, Jim is a **Sales Strategist**. He shows salespeople how to increase sales, earn more money, have more fun, and how to do it all in less time. **His focus is on No-Brainer Selling Skills that get immediate results**.

He is a charter member of Master Speakers International. He has authored five books including the recently published **"57 Ways To Take Control Of Your Time And Your Life"**.

He also has a 7 CD Album called **"How To Get Surefire Selling Results During Tough Times"** and a 6 CD Album called, **"57 Ways To Take Control Of Your Time And Your Life."**

16 years . . . 458 clients . . . 68% repeat business